'What matters is
to live everything.
Live the questions
for now.'

RAINER MARIA RILKE
Born 1875, Prague, Czech Republic
Died 1926, Montreux, Switzerland

Letters to a Young Poet was first published in 1929. This edition
is taken from *Letters to a Young Poet & The Letter from the Young
Worker* translated by Charlie Louth, Penguin Classics, 2011.

RILKE IN PENGUIN CLASSICS
The Notebooks of Malte Laurids Brigge
Selected Poems
Letters to a Young Poet & The Letter from the Young Worker

RAINER MARIA RILKE

Letters to a Young Poet

Translated by
Charlie Louth

PENGUIN BOOKS

PENGUIN CLASSICS

UK | USA | Canada | Ireland | Australia
India | New Zealand | South Africa

Penguin Classics is part of the Penguin Random House group of companies
whose addresses can be found at global.penguinrandomhouse.com.

This selection published in Penguin Classics 2016

007

Translation copyright © Charlie Louth, 2011

The moral right of the translator has been asserted

Set in 9.5/13 pt Baskerville 10 Pro
Typeset by Jouve (UK), Milton Keynes
Printed and bound in Great Britain by Clays Ltd, Elcograf S.p.A.

A CIP catalogue record for this book is available from the British Library

ISBN: 978-0-241-25205-5

www.greenpenguin.co.uk

Preface

In late autumn 1902 it was – I was sitting under ancient chestnut trees in the gardens of the Military Academy in Wiener Neustadt with a book. I was so absorbed by my reading that I hardly noticed it when the only one of our teachers who was not an army officer, Horaček, the learned and good-natured chaplain of the Academy, came and joined me. He took the volume from my hand, looked at the cover and shook his head. 'Poems by Rainer Maria Rilke?' he asked thoughtfully. He leafed through its pages, ran his eyes over a few verses, looked reflectively into the distance and finally nodded. 'So, our pupil René Rilke has become a poet.'

And I was told about the slight, pale boy sent by his parents more than fifteen years before to the Military Lower School in Sankt Pölten so that he might later become an officer. In those days Horaček had worked there as the chaplain and he still remembered his former pupil well. He described him as a quiet, serious, highly gifted child, who liked to keep himself to himself, put up with the discipline of boarding-school life patiently and after the fourth year moved on with the others to the Military Upper School in Mährisch-Weisskirchen. There his constitution proved not to be resilient enough, and so his parents took him out of the establishment and had him continue his studies at

1

home in Prague. What path his career had taken after that Horaček was unable to say.

Given all this it is probably not difficult to understand that I decided that very hour to send my poetic efforts to Rainer Maria Rilke and ask him for his verdict. Not yet twenty years old and on the verge of going into a profession which I felt was directly opposed to my true inclinations, I thought that if anyone was going to understand my situation it was the author of the book To Celebrate Myself. *And without its being my express intention, my verses were accompanied by a letter in which I revealed myself more unreservedly than to anyone ever before, or to anyone since.*

Many weeks went by before an answer came. The letter with its blue seal bore a Paris postmark, weighed heavy in the hand and displayed on the envelope the same clarity, beauty and assurance of hand with which the content itself was written from the first line to the last. And so my regular correspondence with Rainer Maria Rilke began, lasting until 1908 and then gradually petering out because life forced me into domains which the poet's warm, tender and moving concern had precisely wanted to protect me from.

But that is unimportant. The only important thing is the ten letters that follow, important for the insight they give into the world in which Rainer Maria Rilke lived and worked, and important too for many people engaged in growth and change, today and in the future. And where a great and unique person speaks, the rest of us should be silent.

Franz Xaver Kappus
Berlin, June 1929

Dear Sir,

Your letter only reached me a few days ago. Let me thank you for the great and endearing trust it shows. There is little more I can do. I cannot go into the nature of your verses, for any critical intention is too remote from me. There is nothing less apt to touch a work of art than critical words: all we end up with there is more or less felicitous misunderstandings. Things are not all as graspable and sayable as on the whole we are led to believe; most events are unsayable, occur in a space that no word has ever penetrated, and most unsayable of all are works of art, mysterious existences whose life endures alongside ours, which passes away.

Having begun with this preliminary remark, all I will go on to say is that your verses have no identity of their own, though they do have tacit and concealed hints of something personal. I feel that most clearly in the last poem, 'My Soul'. There something individual is trying to come into words, to find its manner. And in the lovely poem 'To Leopardi' perhaps a kind of affinity with this great and solitary man develops. Still, the poems are not yet anything in themselves, nothing self-sufficient, not even the last one and the one to Leopardi. The kind letter you wrote accompanying them does not fail to make many of the shortcomings I sensed in reading your verses explicable, without for all that being able to give them a name.

You ask whether your verses are good. You ask me that. You have asked others, before. You send them to magazines. You compare them with other poems, and you worry when certain editors turn your efforts down. Now (since you have allowed me to offer you advice) let me ask you to give up all that. You are looking to the outside, and that above all you should not be doing now. Nobody can advise you and help you, nobody. There is only one way. Go into yourself. Examine the reason that bids you to write; check whether it reaches its roots into the deepest region of your heart, admit to yourself whether you would die if it should be denied you to write. This above all: ask yourself in your night's quietest hour: *must* I write? Dig down into yourself for a deep answer. And if it should be affirmative, if it is given to you to respond to this serious question with a loud and simple '*I must*', then construct your life according to this necessity; your life right into its most inconsequential and slightest hour must become a sign and witness of this urge. Then approach nature. Then try, like the first human being, to say what you see and experience and love and lose. Don't write love poems; avoid at first those forms which are too familiar and habitual: they are the hardest, for you need great maturity and strength to produce something of your own in a domain where good and sometimes brilliant examples have been handed down to us in abundance. For this reason, flee general subjects and take refuge in those offered by your own day-to-day life; depict your sadnesses and desires, passing thoughts and faith in some kind of beauty – depict all this with intense, quiet, humble sincerity and make use of whatever you find about you to express yourself, the images from your dreams and the things in your memory. If your everyday life seems to lack material, do not blame it; blame yourself, tell yourself that you are not poet enough to summon up its riches, for there is no lack for him who creates and no poor, trivial place. And even if you were in a prison whose walls did not let any of the sounds of the world outside reach your senses – would you not have your childhood still, this marvellous, lavish source, this treasure-house of memories? Turn your attention towards that. Attempt to raise the sunken sensations of this distant past; your self will become the stronger for it, your loneliness will open up and become a twilit dwelling in which the noise other people make is only heard far off. And if from this turn inwards, from this submersion in your own world, there come *verses*, then it will not occur to you to ask anyone whether they are good verses. Nor will you attempt to interest magazines in these bits of work: for in them you will see your beloved natural possessions, a piece, and a voice, of your life. A work of art is good if it has arisen out of necessity. The verdict on it lies in this nature of its origin: there is no other. For this reason, my

5

dear Sir, the only advice I have is this: to go into yourself and to examine the depths from which your life springs; at its source you will find the answer to the question of whether you *have* to write. Accept this answer as it is, without seeking to interpret it. Perhaps it will turn out that you are called to be an artist. Then assume this fate and bear it, its burden and its greatness, without ever asking after the rewards that may come from outside. For he who creates must be a world of his own and find everything within himself and in the natural world that he has elected to follow.

But perhaps even after this descent into yourself and into your solitariness you will have to give up the idea of becoming a poet (the feeling that one could live without writing is enough, as I said, to make it something one should never do). But even then, to have taken pause in the way I am asking you to will not have been in vain. Whatever happens, your life will find its own paths from that point on, and that they may be good, productive and far-reaching is something I wish for you more than I can say.

What else should I say to you? I think everything has been emphasized as it should be; and all I wanted to do in the end was advise you to go through your development quietly and seriously; you cannot disrupt it more than by looking outwards and expecting answers from without to questions that only your innermost instinct in your quietest moments will perhaps be able to answer.

I was delighted to find Professor Horaček's name in your letter; I retain a great admiration for this kind-hearted scholar, a gratitude that has endured over the years. Could you please pass on these sentiments to him; it is very kind of him still to remember me, and I much appreciate it.

The verses you were so good as to entrust me with I am sending back to you along with this letter. Thank you again for the extent and the warmth of your trust – as well as I can, I have attempted with this sincere reply to make myself a little worthier of it than, as a stranger, I really am.

With all devotion and sympathy,
   Rainer Maria Rilke

You must forgive me, my dear Sir, for only attending to your letter of 24 February today: the whole time I have been under the weather, not ill exactly but oppressed by an influenza-like feebleness which has made me incapable of anything. And in the end, when all else had failed, I travelled down to this southern coast, whose beneficial effects have helped me in the past. But I'm still not well again, writing is difficult, and so you must take these few lines as if there were more of them.

First of all you should know that every letter from you will always be a pleasure, and you only need to be understanding with regard to the replies, which often, maybe, will leave you with empty hands; for at bottom, and particularly in the deepest and most important things, we are unutterably alone, and for one person to be able to advise, let alone help, another, a great deal must come about, a great deal must come right, a whole constellation of things must concur for it to be possible at all.

There are just two things I wanted to say to you today:

Irony: don't let yourself be ruled by it, especially not in uncreative moments. In creative ones try to make use of it as one means among many to get a grasp on life. Used purely, it too is pure, and there is no need to be ashamed of it; and if you feel too familiar with it, if you fear your intimacy is growing too much, then turn towards great and serious subjects, next to which irony becomes small and helpless. Seek out the depths of things: irony will never reach down there – and if in so doing you come up against something truly great, inquire whether this way of relating to things originates in a necessary part of your being. For under the influence of serious things irony will either fall away (if it is something incidental) or on the contrary (if it really belongs to you in a native way) it will gain strength and so become a serious tool and take its place among the means with which you will be bound to create your art.

And the second thing I wanted to tell you today is this:

Of all my books there are only a few I cannot do without, and two are always among my effects, wherever I am. I have them with me here: the Bible, and the books of the great Danish writer *Jens Peter Jacobsen*. I wonder whether you know his works. They are easy to get hold of, because a number of them are available in good translations in Reclam's Universal-Bibliothek. Get hold of the little volume *Six Novellas* by J. P. Jacobsen, and his novel *Niels Lyhne*, and begin with the first story in the first of these volumes which is called 'Mogens'. A world will come over you, the joy, the richness, the incomprehensible greatness of a new world. Live in these books for a while, learn from them what seems to be worth learning, but above all love them. This love will be repaid you thousands and thousands of times, and however your life may turn out – this love, I am sure of it, will run through the weave of your becoming as one of the most important threads of all among the other threads of your experiences, disappointments and joys.

If I had to say from whom I have learnt anything about the nature of artistic creation, about its profundity and eternity, there are only two names I can give: *Jacobsen's*, the great, great poet, and *Auguste Rodin's*, the sculptor who has no equal among all artists now alive. –

All success on your paths!

Yours,
Rainer Maria Rilke

Viareggio near Pisa (Italy), 23 April 1903

Your Easter letter, my dear Sir, gave me a great deal of pleasure, for it had many good things to report, and the way you spoke about Jacobsen's great and generous art showed me that I was not mistaken in conducting your life and its many questions to this source of plenty.

Now *Niels Lyhne* will reveal itself to you, a book full of splendours and depths; the more often one reads it, it seems to contain everything, from life's faintest scent to the full, grand savour of its heaviest fruits. There is nothing in it that has not been understood, grasped, lived, and known in memory's trembling, lingering resonance; no experience is too slight, and the merest occurrence unfolds like a fate, and fate itself is like a wonderful, vast fabric in which every thread is drawn by an infinitely tender hand and laid next to another, held in place and supported by a hundred others. You will experience the immense pleasure of reading this book for the first time, and will pass through its innumerable surprises as if in a new dream. But I can tell you that later too one always traverses these books with the same astonishment and that they lose nothing of the wondrous power, relinquish none of the magical qualities, which they lavish on the reader the first time round.

One just takes more and more enjoyment in them, one grows ever more grateful and somehow better and simpler in seeing the world, deeper in one's faith in life and happier and larger in living. –

And later you must read the wonderful book of the fate and longings of *Marie Grubbe* and Jacobsen's letters and diaries and fragments and finally his verse which (even if the translations are only moderate) has an infinite resonance. (To do so, I'd suggest you buy the lovely collected edition of Jacobsen's works – which has all this in it – if you get the opportunity. It came out in three volumes and in good translations with Eugen Diederichs in Leipzig and costs, I believe, only 5 or 6 marks a volume.)

In your opinion on 'Here roses should stand . . .' (a work of such incomparable subtlety and form) you are of course absolutely in the right, and inviolably so, whatever the author of the preface may have to say. And let me at once make this request: read as little as possible in the way of aesthetics and criticism – it will either be partisan views, fossilized and made meaningless in its lifeless rigidity, or it will be neat wordplay, where one opinion will triumph one day and the opposite the next. Works of art are infinitely solitary and nothing is less likely to reach them than criticism. Only love can grasp them and hold them and do them justice. – With regard to any such disquisition, review or introduction, trust yourself and your instincts; even if you go wrong in your judgement, the natural growth of your inner life will gradually, over time, lead you to other insights. Allow your verdicts their own quiet untroubled development which like all progress must come from deep within and cannot be forced or accelerated. *Everything* must be carried to term before it is born. To let every impression and the germ of every feeling come to completion inside, in the dark, in the unsayable, the unconscious, in what is unattainable to one's own intellect, and to wait with deep humility and patience for the hour when a new clarity is delivered: that alone is to live as an artist, in the understanding and in one's creative work.

These things cannot be measured by time, a year has no meaning, and ten years are nothing. To be an artist means: not to calculate and count; to grow and ripen like a tree which does not hurry the flow of its sap and stands at ease in the spring gales without fearing that no summer may follow. It will come. But it comes only to those who are patient, who are simply there in their vast, quiet tranquillity, as if eternity lay before them. It is a lesson I learn every day amid hardships I am thankful for: *patience* is all!

RICHARD DEHMEL: With his books (as also, by the way, with the man himself whom I know slightly) I always find myself, when I've come upon one of his best pages, fearful of the next, which can always undo it all again and turn what was so lovely into something base. You sum him up very well with your phrase about 'living and writing in rut'. – And indeed artistic experience lies so incredibly close to sexual experience, to its pains and pleasures, that both phenomena are really just different forms of one and the same desire and felicity. And if instead of speaking of 'rut' we could say 'sex', sex in the large, capacious, pure sense, not rendered suspect by any misapprehensions stemming from the Church, his art would be very great and infinitely important. His poetic power is immense, as vigorous as instinct; it has its own reckless rhythms running through it and bursts out of him as if from a mountain.

But this power seems not always to be quite genuine and free of affectation. (But then that is one of the severest tests of an artist: he must always remain innocent and unconscious of his greatest virtues if he is to avoid depriving them of their uninhibitedness and purity.) And when this power, coursing through his being, reaches his sexuality, it doesn't find quite the pure human being it needs. The world of sexuality it finds is not entirely mature and pure, it is not *human* enough, only *virile*, rut, intoxication, restlessness, and weighed down by the old prejudices and arrogance with which men have disfigured and overburdened love. Because he loves *only* as a man, not as a human being, there is in his sense of sexuality something narrow, seemingly savage, hateful, time-bound, uneternal that diminishes his art and makes it ambivalent and doubtful. It is not without blemish, it is marked by the times and by passion, and little of it will prevail and endure. (But that's the case with most art!) In spite of all this one can still take deep pleasure in what is great about his work and must just make sure not to lose oneself to it and become an acolyte of this Dehmel-world which is so full of anxiety, of adultery and confusion, and remote from the real destinies, which create more suffering than these passing afflictions but also give more opportunity for greatness and more courage to make something that will last.

To come to my own books, really I'd like to send you all those that might give pleasure. But I am very poor, and as soon as my books have appeared they cease to belong to me. I cannot buy them myself and, as I'd so often like to, give them to those who would value and look after them.

For that reason I have written down for you on a slip of paper the titles (and publishing houses) of my recent books (that is the very newest, altogether I must have published 12 or 13) and must leave it to you, dear Sir, to order one or two of them if they take your fancy.

I shall be glad to know that my books are with you.

All good wishes,

Yours,

Rainer Maria Rilke

About ten days ago I left Paris, ailing and very weary, and travelled to these great northern plains whose vastness and quiet and sky are supposed to return my health to me. But I drove into unceasing rain which only today is beginning to clear a bit over the restless, windswept land; and I'm using this first moment of brightness to send you a greeting, my dear Sir.

My dear Mr Kappus: I have left your letter unanswered for a long time – not that I had forgotten it; on the contrary, it was the kind of letter one reads again, coming across it among one's papers, and I recognized you in it as if I were in your presence. It was your letter of the second of May – I'm sure you remember it. When, as I do now, I read it in the great calm of these expanses, I am touched by your fine concern for life, even more than I was in Paris where everything has a different tone and gets lost in the immense din which sets things trembling. Here, surrounded as I am by a mighty stretch of land over which the winds blow in from seas, here I feel that no human being anywhere can respond to those questions and feelings that have a profound life of their own; for even the best of us get the words wrong when we want them to express such intangible and almost unsayable things. But all the same I believe that you need not remain without solution if you hold to things like those now refreshing my eyes. If you hold close to nature, to what is simple in it, to the small things people hardly see and which all of a sudden can become great and immeasurable; if you have this love for what is slight, and quite unassumingly, as a servant, seek to win the confidence of what seems poor – then everything will grow easier, more unified and somehow more conciliatory, not perhaps in the intellect, which, amazed, remains a step behind, but in your deepest consciousness, watchfulness and knowledge. You are so young, all still lies ahead of you, and I should like to ask you, as best I can, dear Sir, to be patient towards all that is unresolved in your heart and to try to love *the questions themselves* like locked rooms, like books written in a foreign tongue. Do not now strive to uncover answers: they cannot be given you because you have not been able to live them. And what matters is to live everything. *Live* the questions for now. Perhaps then you will gradually, without noticing it, live your way into the answer, one distant day in the future. Perhaps you do carry within yourself the possibility of forming and creating, as a particularly happy and pure way of living. School yourself for it, but take what comes in complete trust, and as long as it is a product of your will, of some kind of inner necessity, accept it and do not despise it. Sex is difficult, true. But difficult things are what we were set to do, almost everything serious is difficult, and everything is serious. If you only acknowledge this and manage from your own resources, from your own disposition and nature, from your own experience and childhood and strength, to win your way towards a relationship to sex that is wholly your own (*not* influenced by convention and custom), then you have no need to fear losing yourself and becoming unworthy of your best possession.

Physical desire is a sensual experience, no different from pure contemplation or the pure sensation with which a fine fruit sates the tongue; it is a great and endless feeling which is granted to us, a way of knowing the world, the fullness and the splendour of all knowledge. And that we receive this pleasure cannot be a bad thing; what is bad is the way almost all of us misuse the experience and waste it and apply it as a stimulus to the tired parts of our lives, as a distraction instead of as a concentration of ourselves into climactic points. Eating, too, has been turned away from its true nature: want on the one hand and superfluity on the other have troubled the clarity of this need, and all the profound, simple necessities in which life renews itself have similarly been obscured. But the individual can clarify them for himself and live in this clearness (and if not the individual, who is too dependent, then at least the solitary). He can remind himself that all beauty in plants and animals is a quiet and durable form of love and longing, and he can see the animal, as also the plant, patiently and willingly joining and multiplying and growing, not from physical pleasure, not from physical suffering, but bowing to necessities which are greater than pleasure and pain and more power-ful than desire and resistance. Oh if only mankind could embrace this mystery, which penetrates the earth right into its smallest elements, with more humility, and bear and sustain it with more gravity and know how ter-ribly heavy it is, instead of taking it lightly. If only mankind could hold its own fertility in awe, which is one and the same whether it manifests itself in the spirit or in the flesh. For creativity of the spirit has its origin in the physical kind, is of one nature with it and only a more delicate, more rapt and less fleeting version of the carnal sort of sex. 'The desire to be a creator, to engender, to give form' is nothing without its continuing, palpable confirmation and realization in the world, nothing with-out the myriad expressions of assent coming from animals and things. And the pleasure it gives is only as unutter-ably fine and abundant as it is because it is full of inherited memories of the engendering and bearing of millions. In one creative thought a thousand forgotten nights of love revive and lend it grandeur and height. And those who come together in the night-time and are entwined in a cradle of desire are carrying out a serious work in collecting sweetness, profundity and strength for the song of some poet yet to come, who will rise up to speak unutterable pleasures. And they summon up the future; and even if they err and embrace one another blindly, the future will come all the same, a new creature will appear, and based on the chance act that seems to be accomplished here the law comes into being according to which a resistant and vigorous seed forces its way through to the egg moving forward to receive it. Do not be distracted by surfaces; it is in the depths that all laws obtain. And those who live the mystery falsely and badly (and there are many of them) forfeit it only for themselves and still hand it on like a sealed letter, unwittingly. And don't be put off by the multiplicity of names and the complexity of the various cases. Perhaps a great maternity lies over everything, as a shared longing. The beauty of the virgin, of a being, who, as you put it so well, 'has not yet achieved anything', is maternity divining and preparing itself, anxious and full of longing. And the beauty of a mother is maternity at work, and that of the old woman a great memory. And in the man too there is maternity, as it seems to me, physical and spiritual; his engendering is also a kind of giving birth, and it is an act of birth when he creates out of his inmost resources. And perhaps the sexes are more closely related than we think, and the great renewal of the world will perhaps consist in man and woman, freed of all sense of error and disappointment, seeking one another out not as opposites but as brothers and sisters and neighbours, and they will join together as *human beings*, to share the heavy weight of sexuality that is laid upon them with simplicity, gravity and patience.

But everything which one day will perhaps be possible for many, the solitary individual can prepare for and build now with his hands which are more unerring. For this reason, dear Mr Kappus, love your solitude and bear the pain it causes you with melody wrought with lament. For the people who are close to you, you tell me, are far away, and that shows that you are beginning to create a wider space around you. And if what is close is far, then the space around you is wide indeed and already among the stars; take pleasure in your growth, in which no one can accompany you, and be kind-hearted towards those you leave behind, and be assured and gentle with them and do not plague them with your doubts or frighten them with your confidence or your joyfulness, which they cannot understand. Look for some kind of simple and loyal way of being together with them which does not necessarily have to alter however much you may change; love in them a form of life different from your own and show understanding for the older ones who fear precisely the solitude in which you trust. Avoid providing material for the drama which always spans between parents and their children; it saps much of the children's strength and consumes that parental love which works and warms even when it does not comprehend. Ask no advice of them and reckon with no understanding; but believe in a love which is stored up for you like an inheritance, and trust that in this love there is a strength and a benediction out of whose sphere you do not need to issue even if your journey is a long one.

It is good that for the moment you are going into a profession which will make you independent and mean you only have yourself to rely on, in every sense. Have the patience to wait and see whether your inmost life feels confined by the form of this occupation. I consider it a very difficult and a very demanding one, as it is burdened by powerful conventions and leaves almost no room to interpret its duties according to your own lights. But your solitude, even in the midst of quite foreign circumstances, will be a hold and a home for you, and leading from it you will find all the paths you need. All my good wishes are ready to accompany you, and you have all my confidence and trust.

Yours,

Rainer Maria Rilke

My dear Sir,

Your letter of 29 August reached me in Florence, and only now – two months on – do I give you news of it. Forgive me this delay, but I prefer not to write letters when I'm travelling because letter-writing requires more of me than just the basic wherewithal: some quiet and time on my own and a moment when I feel relatively at home.

We arrived in Rome about six weeks ago, at a time when it was still the empty, hot city, the Rome supposedly ridden with fevers, and this circumstance, together with other practical difficulties to do with settling in, meant that the unrest surrounding us went on and on and the foreignness of the place lay on us with the weight of homelessness. On top of that you have to remember that Rome (if one is not yet acquainted with it) seems oppressively sad when one first arrives: the lifeless and drear museum-atmosphere it breathes, the abundance of fragments of the past (on which a tiny present nourishes itself) that have been fetched out of the ground and laboriously maintained, the unspeakable excess of esteem, nourished by academics and philologists with the help of run-of-the-mill tourists, given to all these disfigured and spoilt objects which after all are basically nothing more than accidental vestiges of another age and of a life that is not our own and is not meant to be. At last, after weeks of daily fending off, you get your bearings back, and somewhat dazed you tell yourself: No, there is not *more* beauty here than elsewhere, and all these objects which generation after generation have continued to admire, which inexpert hands have mended and restored, they mean nothing, are nothing and have no heart and no value; but there is a great deal of beauty here, because there is beauty everywhere. Infinitely lively waters go over the old aqueducts into the city and on the many squares dance over bowls of white stone and fill broad capacious basins and murmur all day and raise their murmur into the night, which is vast and starry and soft with winds. And there are gardens here, unforgettable avenues and flights of steps, steps conceived by Michelangelo, steps built to resemble cascades of flowing water – giving birth to step after broad step like wave after wave as they descend the incline. With the help of such impressions you regain your composure, win your way back out of the demands of the talking and chattering multitude (how voluble it is!), and you slowly learn to recognize the very few things in which something everlasting can be felt, something you can love, something solitary in which you can take part in silence.

I'm still living in the city, on the Capitol, not far from the finest equestrian statue that has come down to us from Roman art – that of Marcus Aurelius. But in a few weeks I shall be moving into a quiet, simple room, an old summer-house lost in the depths of a great park, hidden away from the city with its noise and its inconsequentiality. I'll live there for the whole winter and take pleasure in the great stillness from which I expect the gift of good and productive hours . . .

From there, where I shall feel more at home, I'll write you a longer letter in which I'll also have something to say about your writing. Today I must just mention (and it was perhaps wrong of me not to have done so before) that the book you announced in your letter (which you said contained pieces by you) has not arrived here. Has it been sent back to you, perhaps from Worpswede? (For: packets cannot be forwarded abroad.) This is the best explanation, which it would be nice to have confirmed. I hope it has not gone astray, which given the Italian postal service cannot be ruled out – alas.

I should have been glad to receive the book (as with everything that gives some sign of you); and any verse you have written since I shall always (if you entrust me with it) read and reread and take in as well and as completely as I can. With good wishes and greetings,

Yours,

Rainer Maria Rilke

My dear Mr Kappus,

You shall not go without greetings from me at Christmas time, when you are perhaps finding your solitude harder than usual to bear among all the festivities. But if you notice that it is great, then be glad of it; for what (you must ask yourself) would a solitude be that was not great? There is only *one* solitude, and it is vast and not easy to bear and almost everyone has moments when they would happily exchange it for some form of company, be it ever so banal or trivial, for the illusion of some slight correspondence with whoever one happens to come across, however unworthy . . . But perhaps those are precisely the hours when solitude grows, for its growth is painful like the growth of boys and sad like the beginning of spring. But that must not put you off. What is needed is this, and this alone: solitude, great inner loneliness. Going into oneself and not meeting anyone for hours – that is what one must arrive at. Loneliness of the kind one knew as a child, when the grown-ups went back and forth bound up in things which seemed grave and weighty because they looked so busy, and because one had no idea what they were up to.

And when one day you realize that their preoccupations are meagre, their professions barren and no longer connected to life, why not continue to look on them like a child, as if on something alien, drawing on the depths of your own world, on the expanse of your own solitude, which itself is work and achievement and a vocation? Why wish to exchange a child's wise incomprehension for rejection and contempt, when incomprehension is solitude, whereas rejection and contempt are ways of participating in what, by precisely these means, you want to sever yourself from?

Think, dear Mr Kappus, of the world that you carry within you, and call this thinking whatever you like. Whether it is memory of your own childhood or longing for your own future – just be attentive towards what rises up inside you, and place it above everything that you notice round about. What goes on in your innermost being is worth all your love, this is what you must work on however you can and not waste too much time and too much energy on clarifying your attitude to other people. Who says you have such an attitude at all? – I know, your profession is hard and goes against you, and I had foreseen your complaints and knew they would come. Now that they have come I cannot assuage them; I can only advise you to consider whether all professions are not like that, full of demands, full of hostility for the individual, steeped as it were in the hatred of those who with sullen resentment have settled for a life of sober duty. The station you are now obliged to occupy is no more heavily burdened with conventions, prejudices and misapprehensions than any other, and if there are some domains that make a show of greater freedom there are none that are vast and spacious and in contact with the great things of which real life consists. Only the solitary individual is subject, like a thing, to the fundamental laws, and if someone goes out into the morning as it is breaking, or looks out into the evening full of occurrence, and if he feels what is happening there, every hint of station slips from him as if from a dead man, although he is standing in the midst of life itself. Dear Mr Kappus, something similar to what you now have to undergo as an officer would have affected you in any of the existing professions, and even if, outside of any position, you had sought only fleeting and non-committal contact with society, you would not have been spared this feeling of constraint. – It is the same everywhere; but that is no reason for anxiety or sadness; if there is no communal feeling between you and other people, try to be near to things – they will not abandon you. The nights are still there and the winds that go through the trees and over the many lands; among things and among animals all is still full of happenings in which you can take part; and the children are still as you were when you were a child, just as sad and happy, and whenever you think of your childhood you live among them again, among the lonely children, and adults are nothing and their dignity has no worth.

And if it frightens and pains you to think of your childhood and of the simplicity and stillness that go together with it, because you can no longer believe in God, who is everywhere present in it, then ask yourself, dear Mr Kappus, whether you have really lost God after all? Is it not rather the case that you have never yet possessed him? For when was it supposed to have been? Do you think a child can hold him, him whom grown men only bear with difficulty and whose weight bows down the old? Do you believe that anyone who really has him could lose him like a little pebble, or don't you think that whoever had him could only be lost by him alone? – But if you acknowledge that he was not present in your childhood, and not before that, if you suspect that Christ was deceived by his longing and Mohammed betrayed by his pride, and if you feel with horror that even now he is not present, at the moment when we are talking about him, what then gives you the right to miss him who never was, as if he had disappeared, and to search for him as if he were lost?

Why don't you think of him as a coming god, who since eternity has lain ahead of us, the future one, the eventual fruit of a tree of which we are the leaves? What prevents you from casting his birth out into the times of becoming and from living your life like a painful and beautiful day in the history of a great pregnancy? Don't you see how everything that happens is always a beginning again, and could it not be *His* beginning, given that beginnings are in themselves always so beautiful? If he is the complete being, must not slighter things come before him, so that he can pick himself out of fullness and abundance? – Must he not be the last in order to encompass all things in himself, and what significance would we have if the one whom we hanker for had already been?

As the bees collect honey together, so we fetch the sweetness out of everything and build *Him*. We begin with the very slightest things, with what is barely noticeable (as long as it comes about through love), with our work and the repose that comes after, with a moment of silence or with a small solitary joy, with everything that we do on our own without helpers and accomplices, we begin him whom we shall never know, just as our ancestors could not live to know us. And yet they are in us, these people long since passed away, as a disposition, as a load weighing on our destinies, as a murmur in the blood and as a gesture that rises up out of the depths of time.

Is there anything that can strip you of the hope of dwelling one day in him, the most remote, the most extreme?

Dear Mr Kappus, celebrate Christmas in the piety of the feeling that He perhaps requires of you precisely this existential anxiety in order to begin. Precisely these days of transition are perhaps the period when everything in you is working on him, just as before, as a child, you worked on him with bated breath. Be patient and even-tempered and remember that the least we can do is not make his becoming more difficult than the earth makes it for spring when it decides to come.

And I wish you happiness and confidence.

Yours,

Rainer Maria Rilke

My dear Mr Kappus,

Much time has gone past since I received your last letter. Don't hold that against me; first it was work, then disruptions and finally ill-health that kept me from replying, whereas I wanted to write to you out of good, peaceful days. Now I feel a little better again (even here the beginning of spring with its bad and fickle transitions was hard to bear) and can manage to send you greetings, dear Mr Kappus, and (as I am very glad to do) say this and that about your letter, as best I can.

You will see: I have copied out your sonnet because I found that it had beauty and simplicity and a native form in which it unfolds with such quiet propriety. It is the best of the verses of yours I have been permitted to read. And I'm giving you this copy now because I know that it is important and a whole new experience to come across a work of one's own in a foreign hand. Read the lines as if they were unknown to you, and you will feel in your inmost self how very much they are yours. –

It has been a pleasure for me to read this sonnet and your letter, which I did often. I thank you for both.

And you must not let yourself be diverted out of your solitude by the fact that something in you wants to escape from it. Precisely this desire, if you use it calmly and judiciously, as a kind of tool, will help you to extend your solitude over a greater expanse of ground. People have tended (with the help of conventions) to resolve everything in the direction of easiness, of the light, and on the lightest side of the light; but it is clear that we must hold to the heavy, the difficult. All living things do this, everything in nature grows and defends itself according to its kind and is a distinct creature from out of its own resources, strives to be so at any cost and in the face of all resistance. We know little, but that we must hold fast to what is difficult is a certainty that will never forsake us. It is good to be alone, for solitude is difficult; that something is difficult should be one more reason to do it.

To love is also good, for love is hard. Love between one person and another: that is perhaps the hardest thing it is laid on us to do, the utmost, the ultimate trial and test, the work for which all other work is just preparation. For this reason young people, who are beginners in everything, do not yet *know* how to love: they must learn. With their whole being, with all their strength, concerted on their solitary, fearful, upward beating hearts, they have to learn to love. An apprenticeship though is always a long, secluded period, and love too is for a great long time and far into life: solitariness, heightened and deepened loneliness for the one in love. Love at first has nothing to do with unfolding, abandon and uniting with another person (for what would be the sense in a union of what is unrefined and unfinished, still second order?);

for the individual it is a grand opportunity to mature, to become something in himself, to become a world, to become a world in himself for another's sake; it is a great immoderate demand made upon the self, something that singles him out and summons him to vast designs. Only in this sense, as a duty to work on themselves ('to hearken and to hammer day and night'), should young people use the love that is given them. The unfolding, the abandon and any kind of togetherness is not for them (who for a long time yet will have to scrimp and save). They are the culmination, and perhaps that for which a human life now is hardly sufficient.

But there young people so often and so badly go wrong: in that they (who by nature have no patience) fling themselves at one another when love comes over them, scatter themselves just as they are in all their troubledness, disorder, confusion ... But what can come of that? What is life supposed to do with this heap of half-broken things that they call their togetherness and would like to call their happiness, were it possible, their future? Each person loses himself then for the other's sake and loses the other and many more who were yet to come. And loses the expanses and possibilities, exchanges the nearing and fleeing of delicate, mysterious things for a sterile helplessness of which nothing more can come; nothing but a bit of disgust, disappointment and deprivation and the escape into one of the many conventions which like public shelters are set up in great numbers along this most dangerous of paths. No area of human experience is so well furnished with conventions as this: there are lifebelts of the most various invention, dinghies and buoyancy devices; society in its wisdom has found ways of constructing refuges of all kinds, for since it has been disposed to make the love-life a pastime, it has also felt obliged to trivialize it, to make it cheap, risk-free and secure, as public pleasures usually are.

It is true that many young people who love wrongly, that is, simply with abandon and not in solitude (and your average person will never move beyond this), feel the oppression of having failed at something and do want to make the state into which they have got liveable and productive in their own, personal way; for their nature tells them that questions of love, even less than all other important matters, cannot be solved publicly and by following this or that consensus; that they are questions that touch the quick of what it is to be human and which in every case require a new, particular and *purely* private response: but how can people who have already flung together and no longer set themselves any limits or tell one another apart, and who therefore possess nothing of their own any more, how on earth can they find a way out of themselves, out of the depths of a solitude that has already been spilt and squandered?

They act out of a shared helplessness, and if they do their best to escape the convention they happen to have noticed (as marriage for example), they fall into the clutches of a less obvious but just as deadly conventional solution; for all around them there is nothing but – convention; when an action derives from a precipitately arrived at and unwitting union, it is *always* conventional; every relationship which is the product of such confusion has its conventions, however unusual (that is, immoral in the generally accepted sense) it may be; yes, even separation would in such a case be a conventional step, an impersonal, fortuitous decision without force and without point.

Whoever looks at the matter seriously finds that, as for death, which is difficult, no explanation, no solution, has yet been discovered for love, which is difficult too: there are no directions, no path. And for these two problems that we carry round with us in a sealed packet and hand on without opening, it will always be impossible to locate a common rule, resting on consensus. But to the same extent that we begin as individuals to venture onto life, these great things will encounter us, on our own, at ever closer quarters. The demands that the hard work of love makes on our development are larger than life, and as beginners we are not a match for them. But if we can hold out and take this love upon us as a burden and an apprenticeship, instead of losing ourselves in all the trivial and frivolous games behind which people have hidden from the utter seriousness of their existence, then perhaps a small advance and some relief will be sensible to those who come long after us. That would mean a great deal.

We are only now just coming to the point where we can consider the relationship of one human individual to another objectively and without prejudice, and our attempts to live such a relation have no model to go on. And yet in the shifting of the times there are already a few things that can help our tentative beginnings.

Girls and women, in their new, particular unfolding, will only in passing imitate men's behaviour and misbehaviour and follow in male professions. Once the uncertainty of such transitions is over it will emerge that women have only passed through the spectrum and the variety of those (often laughable) disguises in order to purify their truest natures from the distorting influences of the other sex. Women, in whom life abides and dwells more immediately, more fruitfully and more trustingly, are bound to have ripened more thoroughly, become more human human beings, than a man, who is all too light and has not been pulled down beneath the surface of life by the weight of a bodily fruit and who, in his arrogance and impatience, undervalues what he thinks he loves. This humanity which inhabits woman, brought to term in pain and humiliation, will, once she has shrugged off the conventions of mere femininity through the transformations of her outward status, come clearly to light, and men, who today do not yet feel it approaching, will be taken by surprise and struck down by it. One day (there are already reliable signs which speak for it and which begin to spread their light, especially in the

37

northern countries), one day there will be girls and women whose name will no longer just signify the opposite of the male but something in their own right, something which does not make one think of any supplement or limit but only of life and existence: the female human being.

This step forward (at first right against the will of the men who are left behind) will transform the experience of love, which is now full of error, alter it root and branch, reshape it into a relation between two human beings and no longer between man and woman. And this more human form of love (which will be performed in infinitely gentle and considerate fashion, true and clear in its creating of bonds and dissolving of them) will resemble the one we are struggling and toiling to prepare the way for, the love that consists in two solitudes protecting, defining and welcoming one another.

And one more thing: do not believe that that abundance of love which was once, as a boy, bestowed on you is now lost. Can you tell whether back then great and good desires did not ripen within you, and resolutions which you still live by today? I believe that love remains so strong and powerful in your memory because it was your first deep experience of solitariness and the first inner work that you undertook on your life. – All good wishes to you, dear Mr Kappus!

Yours,

Rainer Maria Rilke

Sonnet

Through my life there trembles unlamenting
suffering dark and deep, without a sigh.
Pure as snow the blossoming of my dreams
consecrates the stillest of my days.

Often though a question's gravity
cuts across my path. I seem to shrink,
pass coldly on as if beside a lake
whose waters are too vast for me to measure.

And then a sadness settles, dim, opaque,
like the grey of pallid summer nights,
shimmered through with stars – now and then – :

love then is what my hands attempt to grasp
because I want to say a prayer whose sounds
my burning mouth, my lips, cannot bring forth . . .

(Franz Kappus)

Borgeby gård, Flädie, Sweden, 12 August 1904

I want to talk to you again for a while, dear Mr Kappus, although I can say almost nothing that is of any help, hardly anything useful. You have had many great sadnesses which have now passed by. And you say that their passing was also hard and upsetting for you. But I ask you to consider whether these great unhappinesses did not rather pass *through* you. Whether much within you has not changed, whether somewhere, in some part of your being, you were not transformed while you were unhappy? The only sorrows which are harmful and bad are those one takes among people in order to drown them out. Like diseases which are treated superficially and inexpertly, they only abate, and after a short pause break out again with more terrible force, and accumulate inside and are life, unlived, rejected, lost life – from which we can die. If it were possible for us to see further than our knowledge reaches, and a little beyond the outworks of our intuitions, perhaps we should then bear our sadnesses with greater assurance than our joys. For they are the moments when something new enters into us, something unknown to us; our feelings, shy and inhibited, fall silent, everything in us withdraws, a stillness settles on us, and at the centre of it is the new presence that nobody yet knows, making no sound.

I believe that almost all our sadnesses are periods of tautening that we experience as numbness because we can no longer hear the stirring of our feelings, which have become foreign to us. Because we are alone with the strange thing that has entered into us; because everything familiar and accustomed is taken away from us for a moment; because we are in the middle of a transition where we cannot stand still. And that is why sadness passes: what is new in us, the thing that has supervened, has entered into our heart, penetrated to its innermost chamber and not lingered even there – it is already in our blood. And we never quite know what it was. One might easily suppose that nothing had happened, but we have altered the way a house alters when a guest enters it. We cannot say who has come, perhaps we shall never know, but there are many indications that it is the future that enters into us like this, in order to be transformed within us, long before it actually occurs. And that is why it is so important to be solitary and attentive when one is sad: because the apparently uneventful and static moment when our future comes upon us is so much closer to life than that other noisy and accidental point when it happens to us as if from the outside. The quieter, the more patient and open we are in our sadness, the deeper and more unerringly the new will penetrate into us, the better we shall acquire it, the more it will be *our* fate, and when one day in the future it 'takes place' (that is, steps out of us towards others) we shall feel related and close to it in our inmost hearts. And that is necessary. It is necessary – and little by little our development will tend in this

41

direction – that nothing alien should happen to us, but only what has long been part of us. We have already had to adjust our understanding of so many theories of planetary motion, and so too we shall gradually learn to recognize that what we call fate originates in ourselves, in humankind, and does not work on us from the outside. Only because so many people did not absorb their fates while they were inhabited by them, and did not make them a part of themselves, only because of this did they fail to recognize what emerged from them. It was so foreign to them that in their confused panic they assumed it must just have entered into them, for they swore never to have found anything of the sort in themselves before. Just as for a long time people were deceived about the movement of the sun, so we are still deceived about the movement of what is to come. The future is fixed, dear Mr Kappus, but we move around in infinite space.

How could things not be difficult for us?

And if we come back to solitude, it grows ever clearer that fundamentally it is not something that one can take or leave. We *are* solitary. It is possible to deceive yourself and act as if it were not the case. That is all. How much better though, to see and accept that that is what we are, and even to take it as our starting-point. If we do, the effect is admittedly one of giddiness; for all the points on which we are accustomed to rest our eyes are taken away from us, there is no longer anything close by, and everything remote is infinitely so. Someone transported from his room, almost without warning and interval, onto the top of a high mountain would feel something like it: he would be virtually destroyed by an unparalleled sense of insecurity, by an exposure to something nameless. He would think he was falling or believe himself to be hurtling out into space or shattered into a thousand pieces: what a monstrous lie his brain would have to invent to rein in and clarify the state of his senses. In the same way all distances, all measurements, alter for the one who becomes solitary; many such changes suddenly take place at once and, as with the man on the mountaintop, unusual imaginings and curious sensations occur which seem to take on dimensions greater than can be tolerated. But it is necessary for us to experience this too. We must accept our existence in as *wide* a sense as can be; everything, even the unheard-of, must be possible within it. That, when you come down to it, is the only kind of courage that is demanded of us: the courage for the oddest, the most unexpected, the most inexplicable things that we may encounter. That human beings have been cowardly in this regard has done life endless harm; the experiences we describe as 'apparitions', the entire so-called 'spirit world', death, all those things so closely akin to us have by our daily rejection of them been forced so far out of our lives that the senses with which we might apprehend them have atrophied. To say nothing of God. But the fear of the inexplicable has not just rendered the individual existence poorer; relations *between* people, too, have been restricted, as it were lifted out of the river-bed of endless possibilities and placed on a deserted bank where nothing happens. For it is not lethargy alone which causes human relationships to repeat themselves in the same old way with such unspeakable monotony in instance after instance; it is the fearful shying away from any kind of new, unforeseeable experience which we think we may not be equal to. But only someone who is ready for anything and rules nothing out, not even the most enigmatic things, will experience the relationship with another as a living thing and will himself live his own existence to the full. For imagining an individual's existence as a larger or smaller room reveals to us that most people are only acquainted with one corner of their particular room, a place by the window, a little area to pace up and down. That way, they have a certain security. And yet the perilous uncertainty that drives the prisoners in Poe's tales to grope out the outlines of their terrible dungeons and so to know the unspeakable horrors of their surroundings, is so much more human. But we are not prisoners. There are no traps or snares set up around us, and there is nothing that should frighten or torment us. We are placed into life as into the element with which we have the most affinity, and moreover we have after thousands of years of adaptation come to resemble this life so closely that if we keep still we can, thanks to our facility for mimicry, hardly be distinguished from all that surrounds us. We have no reason to be mistrustful of our world, for it is not against us. If it holds terrors they are *our* terrors, if it has its abysses these abysses belong to us, if there are dangers then we must try to love them. And if we only organize our life according to the principle which teaches us always to hold to what is difficult, then what now still appears most foreign will become our most intimate and most reliable experience. How can we forget those ancient myths found at the beginnings of all peoples? The myths about the dragons who at the last moment turn into princesses? Perhaps all the dragons in our lives are princesses, only waiting for the day when they will see us handsome and brave? Perhaps everything terrifying is deep down a helpless thing that needs our help.

So, dear Mr Kappus, you shouldn't be dismayed if a sadness rises up in front of you, greater than any you have ever seen before; or if a disquiet plays over your hands and over all your doings like light and cloud-shadow. You must think that something is happening with you, that life has not forgotten you, that it holds you in its hand; it will not let you fall. Why should you want to exclude from your life all unsettling, all pain, all depression of spirit, when you don't know what work it is these states are performing within you? Why do you want to persecute yourself with the question of where it all comes from and where it is leading? You well know you are in a period of transition and want nothing more than to be transformed. If there is something ailing in the way you go about things, then remember that sickness is the means by which an organism rids itself of something foreign to it. All one has to do is help it to be ill, to have its whole illness and let it break out, for that is how it mends itself. There is so much, my dear Mr Kappus, going on in you now. You must be patient as an invalid and trusting as a convalescent, for you are perhaps both. And more than that: you are also the doctor responsible for looking after himself. But with all illnesses there are many days when the doctor can do nothing but wait. And inasfar as you are your own doctor, this above all is what you must do now.

Do not watch yourself too closely. Do not draw over-rapid conclusions from what is happening to you. Simply let it happen. Otherwise you will too readily find yourself looking on your past, which is of course not uninvolved with everything that is going on in you now, reproach-fully (that is, moralistically). But what now affects you from among the divagations, desires and longings of your boyhood is not what you will recall and condemn. The extraordinary circumstances of a solitary and help-less childhood are so difficult, so complicated, exposed to so many influences and at the same time removed from any real life-context, that if a vice enters into it we must not be too quick to call it a vice. We should in general be very careful with names; it is so often the name of a crime which destroys a life, not the nameless and per-sonal act itself, which was perhaps completely necessary to that life and could have been absorbed by it without difficulty. And the expenditure of energy only seems so great because you put too much importance on the victory. It is not victory that is the 'great thing' you think you have achieved, though the feeling itself is not in error. What is great is that there was already something there that you were able to set in place of that deception, something true and real. Without it, your victory would only have been a moral reaction with no further significance, but as it is it has become a segment of your life. Of your life, dear Mr Kappus, which I am thinking of with so many hopes and wishes. Do you remember how this life of yours longed in childhood to belong to the 'grown-ups'? I can see that it now longs to move on from them and is drawn to those who are greater yet. That is why it does not cease to be difficult, but also why it will not cease to grow.

And if I have anything else to say to you it is this: do not think that the person who is trying to console you lives effortlessly among the simple, quiet words that sometimes make you feel better. His life is full of troubles and sadness and falls far short of them. But if it were any different he could never have found the words that he did.

Yours,
Rainer Maria Rilke

Furuborg, Jonsered, Sweden, 4 November 1904

My dear Mr Kappus,

During this time that has passed without a letter I was partly travelling and partly too busy to be able to write. And even today writing is not going to be easy because I have had to write a good number of letters already and my hand is tired. If I had someone to dictate to I'd have plenty to say, but as it is you'll have to make do with just a few words in return for your long letter.

I think of you often, dear Mr Kappus, and with such a concentration of good wishes that really in some way it ought to help. Whether my letters can really be a help to you, well, I have my doubts. Do not say: Yes, they are. Just let them sink in quietly and without any particular sense of gratitude, and let's wait and see what will come of it.

There's not perhaps much purpose in my dealing with the detail of what you wrote, for what I might be able to say about your tendency towards self-doubt or your inability to reconcile your inner and outer life, or about anything else that assails you – it all comes down to what I have said before: the same desire that you might find enough patience in you to endure, and simplicity enough to have faith; that you might gain more and more trust in what is hard and in your own loneliness among other people. And otherwise let life take its course. Believe me: life is right, whatever happens.

And as to feelings: all feelings are pure that focus you and raise you up. An impure feeling is one that only comprises *one* side of your nature and so distorts you. Any thoughts that match up to your childhood are good. Everything that makes *more* of you than you have hitherto been in your best moments is right. Every heightening is good if it occurs in the quick of your bloodstream, if it is not an intoxication, not a troubling but a joy one can see right to the bottom of. Do you understand what I mean?

And your doubts can become a good quality if you *school* them. They must grow to be *knowledgeable*, they must learn to be critical. As soon as they begin to spoil something for you ask them *why* a thing is ugly, demand hard evidence, test them, and you will perhaps find them at a loss and short of an answer, or perhaps mutinous. But do not give in, request arguments, and act with this kind of attentiveness and consistency every single time, and the day will come when instead of being demolishers they will be among your best workers – perhaps the canniest of all those at work on the building of your life.

That is all, dear Mr Kappus, that I can say to you for today. But I'm also sending you the off-print of a little work that has just appeared in the Prague journal *Deutsche Arbeit*. There I continue to speak to you of life and of death and of the greatness and splendour of both.

Yours,

Rainer Maria Rilke

Paris, on the second day of Christmas 1908

You ought to know, dear Mr Kappus, how happy I was to get this lovely letter from you. The news you give me, actual and articulate as it now is, seems good to me, and the more I thought about it the more it struck me as incontrovertibly good. I really wanted to write you this in time for Christmas Eve; but what with the work that has been occupying me variously and without interruption this winter the old festival came up so quickly that I hardly had time enough to make the most necessary purchases, much less to write a letter.

But during these Christmas days I have often thought of you and imagined how quiet you must be in your solitary fort up among the empty mountains over which those great south winds rush as if they wanted to devour them in mighty chunks.

The silence must be immense to be able to receive such sounds and movements, and when one thinks that they are joined by the noise of the sea, present in the distance, perhaps the most inward note in this prehistoric harmony, one can only hope that you have the trust and patience to let this marvellous solitude work on you, a solitude which will never be deleted from your life. In all that lies before you to experience and do, it will continue as an anonymous influence and have a subtly decisive effect, perhaps like the way the blood of our ancestors moves unceasingly within us and mingles with our own to make us the unique, not-to-be-repeated being that we are at every turn of our lives.

Yes: I am glad that you have this firm, utterable form of existence, the rank, the uniform, the duty, all these tangible and well-defined things that in such surroundings, with an equally isolated and not numerous company of men, take on a seriousness and necessity; and which, over and above the aspects of play and pastime that are also part of the military profession, make for a certain vigilance and not only permit an individual attentiveness but actually teach it. And to be in circumstances that work on us, that set us before great natural phenomena from time to time, is all we need.

Art too is only a way of living, and it is possible, however one lives, to prepare oneself for it without knowing; in every real situation we are nearer to it, better neighbours, than in the unreal half-artistic professions which by pretending to be close to art in fact deny and hurt its very existence, as for example is the case with the whole of journalism and almost all criticism and three-quarters of what passes for literature. I am glad, in a word, that you have withstood the dangers of slipping into all this, and that somewhere you are living alone and courageous in a rough reality. May the year to come maintain and strengthen you in it.

Ever yours,
R. M. Rilke